THE NATURE KIDS GUIDE TO
FROGS

DAVID ANDERSON

LP Media Inc. Publishing

For information address LP Media Inc. Publishing,
30012 Variolite St NW, Princeton MN 55371
www.lpmedia.org

Publication Data

Frogs
The Nature Kid's Guide to Frogs — First edition.

Summary: "Learn all about Frogs, the Nature Kid Way"
— Provided by publisher.

ISBN: 979-8-89818-098-0

[1. Frogs – Non-Fiction] I. Title.

Title: The Nature Kid's Guide to Frogs

CONTENTS

WET WORLDS

Some frogs, like the wood frog, can survive being frozen solid in winter. Their hearts stop and they do not breathe. In spring, they thaw out and hop away like nothing happened!

Ribbit! A green frog sits on a lily pad. It watches a fly buzz by.

Frogs live in wet places around the world. They need water to keep their skin moist. Most frogs live near ponds, lakes, or streams. Some live in rainforests where it rains a lot.

Frogs can be found on every continent except Antarctica, which is too cold for them. They like warm and wet habitats best.

Some frogs live in trees, while others burrow underground. A few kinds even live in deserts! These desert frogs hide in the sand until rain comes.

FROGS EVERYWHERE

Splash! A frog dives into a jungle stream. It swims away fast.

Different frog species live all over the world. Some frogs live high in mountains over 16,000 feet up, while others live in steamy jungle valleys near the sea.

Frogs have been on Earth for a long time. They were even hopping around before the dinosaurs!

The most frog species live in tropical areas where it's warm and water is plentiful. Brazil alone has over 1,000 kinds of frogs.

Australia has over 240 frog species. Many live nowhere else on Earth.

TINY FROGS

A tiny Paedophryne frog rests on a penny. It fits with room to spare!

Frogs come in many sizes. The smallest frog is the Paedophryne frog from Papua New Guinea. A Goliath frog can weigh as much as a newborn baby.

Small frogs often live in leaf litter. Their tiny bodies hide well there. Big frogs need more space and food.

Most frogs are somewhere in between. They range from jelly bean-sized to hand-sized.

FUN FACT!

The Goliath frog can move rocks to build its own nesting pools. No other frog does this!

FROG POWER

DID YOU KNOW?
A frog's tongue is attached at the front of its mouth, not the back like ours.

Snap! A red-eyed tree frog grips a branch. Its big toes stick tight.

Red-eyed tree frogs live in rainforests. They sleep during the day on green leaves. Their bright green skin helps them hide. When they close their eyes, they almost disappear!

These frogs have amazing bodies. Their big red eyes scare predators away. Blue and yellow stripes cover their sides. Sticky toe pads help them climb tall trees.

They eat bugs at night. They catch crickets, moths, and flies. Their long, sticky tongue zaps prey in a flash. These colorful frogs are true rainforest acrobats!

SUPER SENSES

Buzz! A frog hears a fly nearby. Its eyes turn to look.

Frogs have amazing senses. A frog's large eyes give it a wide view. This helps them spot movement all around.

Frog ears are round circles behind their eyes. These flat eardrums can pick up sounds in air and water.

Some frogs also feel ground vibrations through their skin. This helps them sense danger coming.

Some frogs have ears bigger than their eyes!

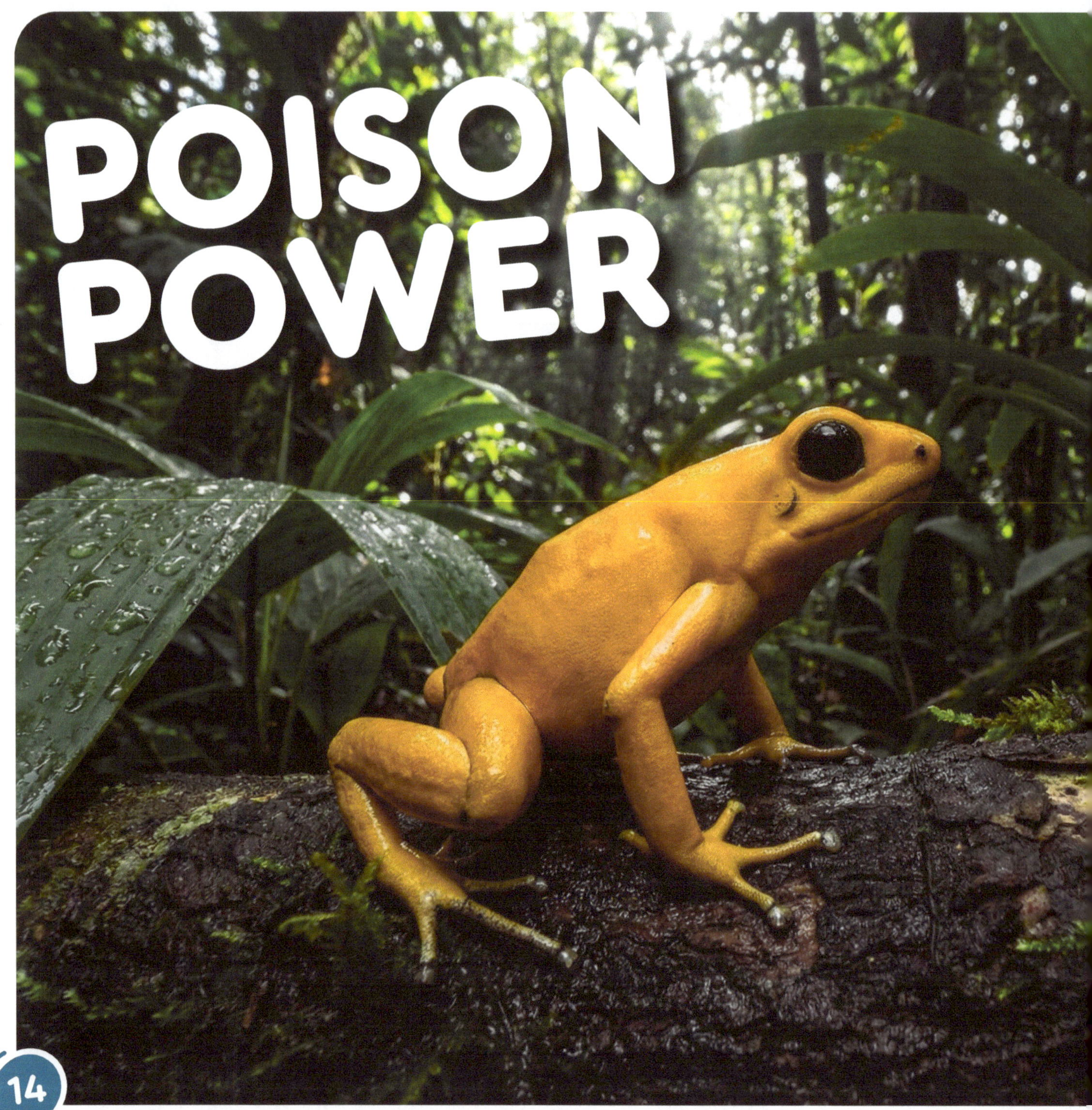

POISON
POWER

A Golden Poison Dart frog sits on a log. Its colors warn predators away.

Some frogs have poison in their skin. Bright colors tell other animals to stay away. Red, yellow, and blue warn predators of danger.

Poison dart frogs are very toxic. One tiny frog has enough poison to harm large animals. These colorful frogs live in the rainforests of Columbia in South America.

The poison comes from the bugs they eat. Most frogs are not poisonous.

Indigenous people used frog poison on hunting darts to catch animals. That's how the Poison Dart frog got it's name!

BUG
BUFFET

Chomp! A bullfrog gulps down a beetle. It looks for more food.

Frogs eat many kinds of bugs. They munch on flies, ants, and beetles. Mosquitoes and gnats are tasty snacks too.

Bigger frogs eat bigger prey. They catch spiders and worms. A few large frogs even eat small mice!

Frogs do not chew their food. They swallow prey whole. Their eyes push down to help food go into their belly.

Sometimes frogs use their front legs to stuff big prey into their mouths!

TONGUE TRAP

Frog spit is like magic. It turns runny to wrap around a bug, then sticky to drag it back into the frog's mouth. No other animal has spit that can do this!

Flick! A frog's tongue shoots out. It grabs a moth.

Frogs catch food with their tongues. A frog's tongue can reach far beyond its mouth. This also lets it flip out very fast.

The tongue is soft and sticky. It works like wet glue. When it hits a bug, the prey sticks tight.

Frogs strike in the blink of an eye. The whole catch takes less than one second. Then the tongue snaps back with the meal.

Frogs sit very still before they strike. This helps them wait for prey to come close. Many frogs have very good aim when they strike.

WATCH OUT

Swoosh! A hawk dives toward a pond. A frog hides fast.

Frogs have many **predators**. Birds, snakes, and fish all hunt them. Even some turtles eat frogs. Life near the pond can be dangerous.

Frogs use tricks to stay safe. They have green or brown skin. This helps them hide in plants and mud. Some frogs can jump very far to escape.

Many frogs are most active at night. The dark helps them hide. They sit still when danger is near.

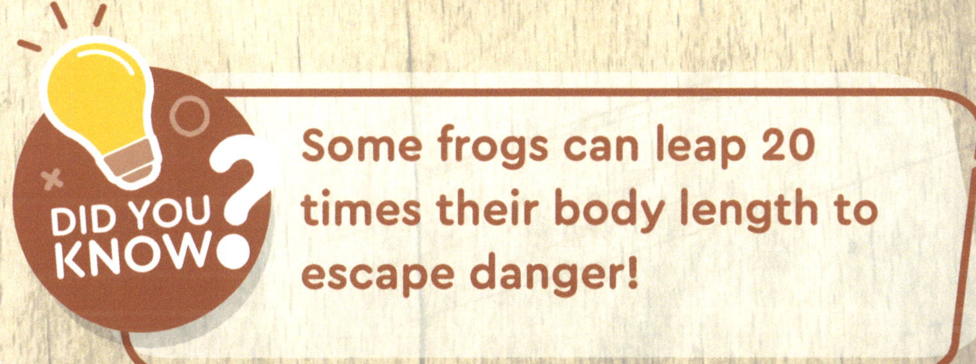

LEAP AWAY

Whoosh! A frog leaps off a rock. It lands in tall grass.

Frogs jump to escape predators. Their strong back legs help them leap far and fast.

Frog legs have powerful muscles. These muscles work like springs. They store energy and release it all at once.

Jumping also helps frogs catch food. They leap toward bugs and snatch them with sticky tongues.

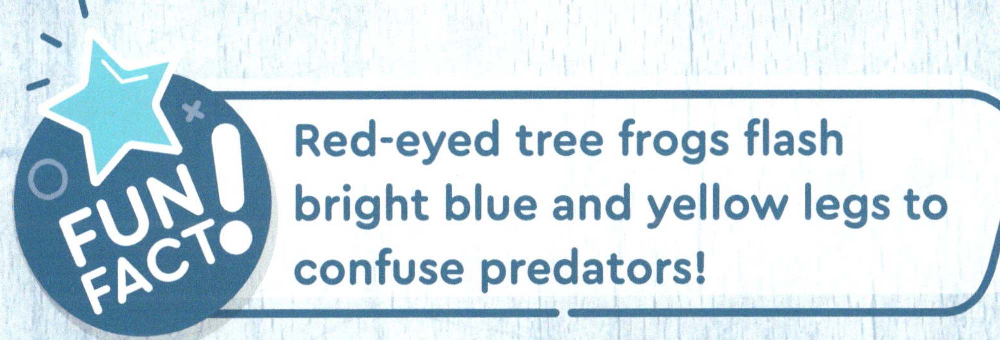

Red-eyed tree frogs flash bright blue and yellow legs to confuse predators!

JUMP IN

Plop! A frog jumps off a lillypad. It kicks its strong legs and swims away.

Frogs move in many ways. They hop on land and swim in water. Their strong back legs do most of the work.

Frog feet are webbed like flippers. The skin between their toes pushes water. This helps frogs glide through ponds.

Some frogs climb trees. Their sticky toe pads grip bark and leaves.

DID YOU KNOW?

The Wallace's Flying Frog can glide through the air by spreading their webbed feet wide like tiny parachutes.

DAILY LIFE

DID YOU KNOW?
Some day-active frogs sunbathe to warm up. They stretch out flat on rocks or leaves to soak up heat!

Chirp! A frog wakes up under a cool leaf. It is time to find a shady spot.

Many frogs rest during the day. They hide under rocks, logs, and leaves. Shade keeps frog skin moist and cool.

Some frogs stay near water all day. They sit in shallow pools or wet mud. These wet spots stop frog skin from drying out.

Some frogs are awake during the day instead of at night. They hunt for food and call out to other frogs in the sunshine.

These daytime frogs often have thicker, waxier skin than other frogs. This special skin keeps moisture in so they don't dry out in the sun. Some even rub a waxy coating over their bodies with their legs to stay moist!

28

Rustle! A frog sits alone in wet grass. It waits for bugs.

Many adult frogs prefer to live alone. Each frog finds its own hiding spot.

Frogs meet other frogs to mate. Males call to females with loud sounds. After **mating**, most frogs go their own way.

Some tadpoles swim together in ponds. But adult frogs spread out. They hunt and hide by themselves.

Some frogs wrestle other frogs that enter their space. They push eachother until one hops away!

CROAKY CALLS

Screech! A male frog puffs up its throat. The loud call fills the night.

Male frogs call to attract females. Each frog species has its own sound. Some peep. Others trill or grunt.

Frogs have **vocal sacs** under their chins. Air moves from the lungs into the sac. The sac swells like a balloon, which makes sound louder.

Females listen for calls. They follow the sounds to find a male. All this calling takes a lot of energy.

The tiny coqui frog is only one inch long, but its call can be heard hundreds of meters away!

32

Tiny black dots wiggle in the water. They are frog eggs.

Many frogs lay their eggs in ponds and streams. A mother frog can lay hundreds of eggs at once. The eggs stick together in a jelly-like clump. This jelly keeps the eggs safe.

After a few days, the eggs hatch into tadpoles. Tadpoles look like tiny fish with long tails. They breathe through gills.

Slowly, the tadpoles change. They grow back legs first, then front legs. Their tails shrink. Soon they become little frogs ready to hop on land.

Only a few tadpoles survive to become frogs. Birds, fish, and snakes eat many of them. Some frogs guard their eggs to help them stay safe.

GROWING UP

DID YOU KNOW?
Some frogs live fifteen years. The oldest frog ever recorded reached forty years old!

Crunch! A young frog catches its first bug. Then it hops away to find more.

Young frogs face many dangers. Birds, fish, and snakes all try to eat them. Out of the thousands of tadpoles only a few survive to become adults.

Most frog parents do not care for their young. They aly the eggs then leave. The tadpoles must grow on their own. This means they must find food and hide from predators.

Some frogs are different. Poison dart frogs carry tadpoles on their backs. They move them to safe pools of water. A few frog species guard their eggs until they hatch.

PONDS VANISH

Rumble! A bulldozer pushes dirt into a pond. Frogs must find new homes.

Frogs need wetlands like ponds, swamps, and marshes to survive. But many of these homes are disappearing.

People drain wetlands to build roads and houses. Without ponds, tadpoles have nowhere to grow into frogs.

Pollution hurts frogs too. They breathe through their thin skin. Polluted air can make them sick.

At least 200 frog species have gone extinct in recent years. Many more may disappear before scientists even discover them.

HELPING
FROGS

Click! A scientist counts frogs in a pond. She writes notes about each one.

Many people work to save frogs. Scientists study them to learn what they need.

Some groups build new ponds for frogs. They also plant trees near streams. This gives frogs safe places to live and lay eggs.

Zoos help rare frogs too. They raise baby frogs and release them into the wild. These efforts give frogs a chance to survive.

Zoos keep Panamanian golden frogs safe. A fungus killed wild ones, so zoos help them survive.

GLOSSARY

Indigenous
People who are the original inhabitants of a land

Mating
When a male and female animal come together to make babies.

predators
Animals that hunt and eat other animals.

Pollution
Harmful substances like trash, chemicals, or dirty water that damage the environment and hurt plants and animals.

vocal sacs
Stretchy pouches in a frog's throat that help make sounds louder.